Asking Questions About How the News Is Created

Carla Mooney

Published in the United States of America by Cherry Lake Publishing
Ann Arbor, Michigan
www.cherrylakepublishing.com

Consultants: Barb Palser, Digital Media Executive; Marla Conn, ReadAbility, Inc.
Editorial direction and book production: Red Line Editorial
Book design: Sleeping Bear Press

Photo Credits: Shutterstock Images, cover, 1, 6, 15; NASA/AP Images, 5; iStockphoto, 9, 16, 19, 20; Andrea Raffin/ Shutterstock Images, 10; iStock/Thinkstock, 12; Eldar Nurkovic/Shutterstock Images, 23; Rowan Staszkiewicz/Press Association/AP Images, 24; Chris Pizzello/AP Images, 26; Simmi Simons/iStockphoto, 28

Library of Congress Cataloging-in-Publication Data

Mooney, Carla, 1970-
  Asking questions about how the news is created / by Carla Mooney.
    pages cm. -- (Asking questions about media)
  Includes bibliographical references and index.
  ISBN 978-1-63362-489-4 (hardcover : alk. paper) -- ISBN 978-1-63362-505-1 (pbk. : alk. paper) -- ISBN 978-1-63362-521-1 (pdf ebook) -- ISBN 978-1-63362-537-2 (hosted ebook)
  1. Television broadcasting of news--Juvenile literature. 2. Journalism--Juvenile literature. 3. Reporters and reporting--Juvenile literature. I. Title.

  PN4784.T4M57 2015
  070.1'95--dc23

                                    2015008950

Cherry Lake Publishing would like to acknowledge the work of
the Partnership for 21st Century Skills. Please visit www.p21.org
for more information.

Printed in the United States of America
Corporate Graphics

ABOUT THE AUTHOR

Carla Mooney is the author of several books for young readers. She is an avid follower of several news programs. A graduate of the University of Pennsylvania, she lives in Pittsburgh, Pennsylvania, with her husband and three children.

TABLE OF CONTENTS

BREAKING NEWS

On July 20, 1969, more than half a billion people huddled around television sets. Breathlessly, they watched a live news **broadcast** that showed astronauts from the Apollo 11 spaceflight land on the moon. Viewers marveled as American astronauts Neil Armstrong and Buzz Aldrin stepped onto the moon's surface. For the first time in history, humans walked on the moon. Through the news, the world was there with them. The broadcast had a long-lasting impact on viewers. Many who watched the landing became

The Apollo 11 moon landing demonstrated to the world the power of broadcast media.

convinced that if humans could walk on the moon, anything was possible.

For generations, people have turned to the news **media** to learn about the world and events around them. The news media focuses on delivering information to the public. It includes print media, such as newspapers and magazines. It delivers broadcast news on the radio and television. On the Internet and social media platforms, news is reported almost as soon as it happens.

People have long relied on the news media to keep them in touch with current events.

No matter what form it takes, the news media has the power to shape people's opinions and views of the world. Reporters cover current events, politics, weather, sports, entertainment, and other events. Through its reports, the news media influences how people think and feel about society.

Every step of creating a news report involves questions. Viewers can investigate the news media world by asking questions of their own:

- Who creates the news, and what motivates them?

- What techniques does the news media use to get my attention?

- Why do people **interpret** the same news story in different ways?

- What points of view are included, and which are left out? Is this a form of **bias**?

We'll explore these questions and more as we look at how the news is made.

REPORTING THE NEWS

Many people work to bring you the news. Reporters, announcers, and anchors report the news. Many more people work behind the scenes. Engineering technicians set up and operate the electrical equipment needed for broadcasts. Photographers and camera operators capture images to tell a story visually. Film and video editors manipulate images. Writers and editors develop content for articles and scripts for broadcast news reports. And the news director supervises the entire news department and determines which stories to run. Each person involved in the process brings his or her own biases and opinions into the decisions that go into creating the news.

CHAPTER 2

CHOOSING THE HEADLINES

Newspapers select the stories that will be front-page news. Television news shows pack many stories into a 30-minute time slot. Even Internet news outlets pick stories to promote on their sites' main pages. So who creates the news and what motivates them?

News companies do not have the time or space to tell you about every event. Before a newspaper is printed, a television news show is aired, or an Internet news site goes live, important decisions are made about the news. These decisions affect what stories people read and see.

Not every story can be front-page news. Media organizations have to decide which stories to report and how much attention they deserve.

Reporters, directors, editors, and others involved in the news creation process all play a role in choosing which stories make the news. When deciding which stories to run, news companies consider several factors. Is the story timely? Is it original? Does the story affect and interest the target audience? Is it controversial? Does it involve a celebrity?

To help them find out what type of stories matter to the audience, news companies do research. TV stations use ratings companies to tell them how many people watch programs and when viewers tune in. Ratings research also tells TV stations the age and gender of their audiences. Radio stations get similar ratings information as well. Internet news sites and newspapers with web editions use online tools to track their audiences. They track the number of visitors to their websites and which pages are viewed the most. By tracking page views, these online news companies can tell which stories are read the most online. They use this

Entertainers and other celebrities get a lot of coverage in the news because they have proven to be popular with readers and viewers.

ENTERTAINMENT VS. HARD NEWS

News outlets often present a mix of hard news and entertainment news. Hard news is about important events that affect people's lives. A local fire or a report on a city council meeting are examples of hard news. Entertainment news includes stories that involve celebrities, television shows, movies, or music. Entertainment news does not affect people's lives, but it can be interesting. Sometimes entertainment news attracts more readers or viewers than hard news. A bigger audience leads to more advertising money.

information to help determine what stories to pursue in the future.

So why do news companies care which stories people want to see and read? News companies want to be the first to report breaking and important news. But they also have another goal. News companies want to make money. Newspapers, magazines, and websites sell space to advertisers. Television and radio stations sell airtime for commercials. News companies that reach more

TV news is often filled with stories about car crashes, natural disasters, and other dramatic events.

people can make more money from advertising.

That's why some news outlets might feature a story about a popular celebrity and give less time or space to another story. If the celebrity story is popular, more people will watch or read it. Those news outlets are likely to keep reporting on it. And they will probably choose similar stories in the future.

So the next time you are watching a television news broadcast or reading a newspaper, ask yourself: Who created the news and what motivates them?

Case Study
Sports, Weather, and Traffic

The types of stories run by local news television broadcasts are changing, according to a 2013 Pew Research Center survey. In the survey, researchers found that stories involving sports, weather, and traffic had grown to fill 40 percent of airtime. The researchers compared local news broadcasts from 2005 to those in late 2012 and early 2013. The time spent on sports stories nearly doubled, from 7 percent in 2005 to 12 percent in 2012. The time spent covering weather and traffic also increased, from 25 percent in 2005 to 29 percent in 2012. In addition, the survey found that 42 percent of local newscasts in 2012–13 began with a weather report or story. Other topics that received increased coverage included accidents, disasters, and unusual events.

At the same time, coverage of other topics in local news has decreased. Crime stories fell from 29 percent in 2005 to 17 percent in 2012. Politics and government stories also decreased from 7 percent of airtime in 2005 to 3 percent in 2012.

CHAPTER 3

GRABBING YOUR ATTENTION

For a news outlet to be successful, people need to read or watch it. News companies want to get your attention fast and keep it. The next time you see a news story, ask yourself what techniques the news media uses to get your attention.

Media outlets often choose high-interest, attention-grabbing headlines. Stories about disasters, such as fires, crimes, and war, attract many people. Stories with an emotional appeal also attract people. A feature about a local child's battle with cancer will draw readers and viewers.

News stories about celebrities also grab people's attention. Think about how many stories you've seen about celebrities, such as the Kardashians. These stories report details including what clothes they wore and where they went. When you watch the news, what types of stories do you notice the most?

Television and radio stations get attention by flashing multiple sound bites of information. A sound bite is a short, catchy comment by a public figure or celebrity that the news outlet replays. Sound

The news media often use stories about celebrities to get your attention.

bites get you interested in a story so that you will keep listening or watching. In a similar way, newspapers and websites use catchy headlines to draw your attention. Engaging headlines attract people to read more.

News companies also use production techniques to grab your attention. Colorful photos, videos, graphics, music, sound effects, and slow motion can attract more viewers. A television report about a blazing fire often

Sound bites from politicians, celebrities, or other newsmakers can draw you into a story or keep your attention.

UP NEXT

News outlets use teases to attract people. A tease is a short advertisement for an upcoming story. News outlets usually tease high-interest stories such as health warnings or weather forecasts. Teases get people's attention and keep them tuned in to the broadcast. They also can be posted on a TV station's website or sent via social media to attract viewers.

includes a music intro, video clips, fancy graphics, and a "Breaking News" bulletin to get viewers to watch. Online, a news outlet might post links to stories on social media sites, such as Twitter and Facebook, to entice you to go to its website.

Television news broadcasts usually feature attractive anchors and reporters. These **charismatic** people appear strong and confident. Viewers are more likely to watch charismatic people report the news.

The same news message can be constructed in different ways. Asking questions about what tools and techniques news outlets use to attract viewers and readers can help you better analyze the message.

CHAPTER 4

INTERPRETING THE MESSAGE

Even when two people watch or read the same news story, they may not feel the same way about the news. Each person may receive a different message from the same story. How does that happen? Why do people interpret the same news story in different ways?

Although a news story has the same **text** for everyone, the **subtext** may be different. The text is what's on the surface. It's the part of the story that everybody sees. The subtext is not seen or heard. It is the meaning that you create from the news story in your mind. Your subtext is based on your past experiences and knowledge. It is also affected by your opinions, attitudes, and values. Everyone has different backgrounds, experiences, and values. Therefore, two

People can have different reactions to the same news story if they interpret the story's subtext differently.

people watching exactly the same news story can interpret it in very different ways.

Several factors may affect how you interpret the news. Your race, gender, and religious beliefs can influence how you think about a news story. Age can also be a factor in how you feel about news stories. For example, a story about increasing taxes to pay for a new

Studies have shown that women remember more details about negative news stories than men.

WOMEN MORE SENSITIVE TO NEGATIVE NEWS

According to a 2012 study by researchers at the University of Montreal, women are more sensitive to negative news stories than men. The scientists found that after viewing the same negative stories, the women had stronger reactions to stressful situations afterward. The women also remembered more details about the negative news than the men remembered. The researchers say it is important to understand that everyone has different reactions to the same news.

senior citizens' center may be seen very differently by a 20-year-old and a 70-year-old. Income status and ethnic background can also play roles in how a person interprets a news story.

Understanding these factors can help you see how a news story may be interpreted by people of different backgrounds. The next time you watch or read the news, think about your reaction to the story. Then consider how the factors from your background may affect your feelings. How might other people interpret the same story?

CHAPTER 5

BIAS IN THE NEWS

Every news story can be told in many ways. When news outlets cover similar stories, they may choose to focus on different details or parts of the story. When watching or reading the news, it is important to understand what points of view are presented. In addition, what points of view are left out of the news media, and is this a form of bias?

Journalists and news directors constantly make decisions about which news stories to run. They also choose which details to include in the story. These decisions can affect the information you get from the news. Sometimes these decisions can create bias.

Bias in the news can be created in several ways. Bias by **omission** occurs when a report leaves out one side of the story or ignores it completely. It presents only facts

Bias can occur when directors and editors make decisions about which stories to report and how to cover them.

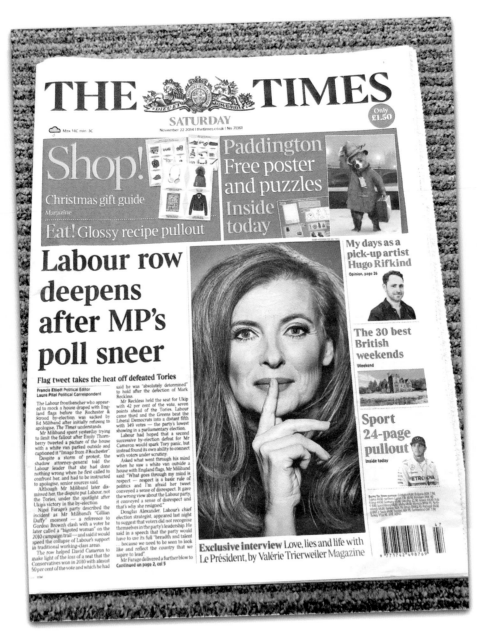

You can often tell which stories a news organization considers important
based on their placement in a newspaper or within a newscast.

SOURCES

Reporters often rely on a **source** to get information on a story. Sources are usually people or organizations that are involved with the story. However, if a reporter chooses to present more sources that favor one side of an issue than the other side, the report may be biased. To analyze whether a story has bias because of source selection, you can ask questions about the backgrounds and affiliations of the people quoted as experts or sources in the story. Are there an equal number of sources on each side of the issue? If not, the story may have a bias.

or reports only stories that support a particular point of view or belief. Bias by omission can occur in a single story. It can also happen over time when a news outlet repeatedly ignores stories or reports only one side of events.

News companies can also create bias through story selection. You can look to see if the outlet highlights stories with a similar point of view or agenda. You can ask yourself if the outlet ignores stories with an opposing view. Do stories with opposing views get equal amounts of coverage? If not, bias may exist.

Placement of news stories can also create bias. Studies have shown that the average newspaper reader

Many cable TV news organizations are often criticized for having a political bias.

mostly scans headlines. Readers will more likely see stories that are placed in a **prominent** position on the page. Stories in less prominent places will be read less. To evaluate placement bias, you can ask where a newspaper or website places stories on different sides of an issue. Are they given similar positions on the page? Or are some stories placed more prominently?

TYPES OF BIAS

Several types of bias can exist in the news. One of the most common forms of bias is political bias. Political bias exists when either liberal or conservative views are featured over the other side. Political bias can occur when a news report is influenced by a reporter's own political views or a news company's views.

Other times, geographic bias occurs when news stories cover events from an American point of view while excluding international points of view. Other controversial subjects that might be affected by bias include race, religion, science and evolution, global warming, and sexual orientation.

Coverage of presidential politics can reveal a bias in the news media.

Sometimes, people see bias even if there is none. This can happen if a person has a hard time accepting other points of view. He or she may have a hard time seeing a report that presents the opposing view as fair.

The news media has an often complicated job to do. It must report the news fairly but also be interesting enough to attract viewers and readers. As a young consumer of the media, you should always ask questions about what you're seeing and hearing and how it affects your daily life.

CABLE NEWS CHANNELS AND BIAS

Cable news networks claim to present **objective** coverage of current events. Yet some channels are widely believed to have a political bias. Fox News Channel is considered to have a conservative bias, while its rival MSNBC is commonly believed to have a liberal bias.

During the 2012 presidential election, the Pew Research Center conducted a study about political bias on these two cable news channels. Researchers followed the networks for an eight-week period. They tracked whether stories about the two presidential candidates were positive or negative in tone. They found that the Democratic candidate, Barack Obama, received far more negative coverage than positive coverage on Fox News. Nearly 46 percent of stories about Obama on Fox were negative, while only 6 percent were positive.

On MSNBC, the researchers found the opposite bias. The Republican candidate, Mitt Romney, received 71 percent negative coverage on the channel. Only 3 percent of the stories about Romney on MSNBC had a positive tone. According to the research, it appears that both channels showed a political bias in their pre-election coverage.

THINK ABOUT IT

When you watch or read the news, think about who chooses the stories to run and which details to include. Who creates the news and what motivates them?

The next time you watch or read the news, notice what catches your attention. What techniques does the news media use to get your attention?

When you see a news story, think about how different people may interpret it. Why do people interpret the same news story in different ways?

As you watch a news story about a controversial topic, ask yourself if the coverage of the issue is fair and balanced. What points of view are left out of the news media, and is this a form of bias?

LEARN MORE

FURTHER READING

Botzakis, Stergios. *What's Your Source? Questioning the News.* Mankato, MN: Capstone Press, 2009.

Palser, Barb. *Choosing News: What Gets Reported and Why.* North Mankato, MN: Compass Point Books, 2012.

WEB LINKS

Center for Media Literacy
www.medialit.org/reading-room/media-literacy-usa
Learn the history of media literacy efforts.

The News Manual
www.thenewsmanual.net/index.htm
An online manual for journalists and people interested in the media.

Newseum
www.newseum.org/
Learn about the history of the media and experience stories of the past and present.

GLOSSARY

bias (BYE-uhs) favoring one person or point of view over another

broadcast (BRAWD-kast) a television or radio program

charismatic (ka-riz-MAT-ik) charming and persuasive

interpret (in-TUR-prit) to decide what something means

media (MEE-dee-uh) different forms of communication that reach a large number of people

objective (uhb-JEK-tiv) influenced by or based on facts, not feelings

omission (oh-MISH-uhn) something that is left out or not disclosed

prominent (PROM-uh-nuhnt) very easily seen

source (sorss) someone or something that provides information

subtext (SUHB-tekst) the underlying meaning of something

text (tekst) the actual words, images, and/or sounds in an advertisement

INDEX